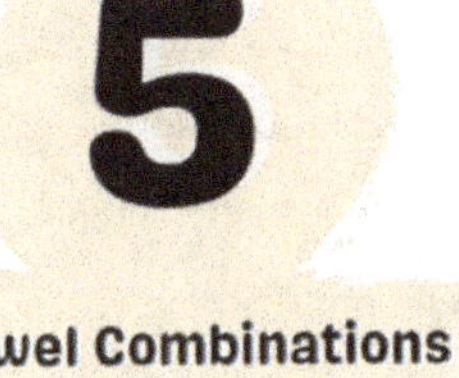



AF351631

# Super Crazy Fun

# BIG KID PHONICS

## WARNING!

## Lots of crazy words!

© Matthew Hitch &
Sunok Moon 2023

Author: Matthew Hitch

Co-author: Sunok Moon

Illustrator: Matthew Hitch

Cover Design: Brittany Hitch

Layout Design: Matthew Hitch

Text Design: Matthew Hitch

Image Manager: Matthew Hitch

~~Vain Meglomaniac: Matthew Hitch~~

Credits Editor: Matthew Hitch

Image Manager Manager: S. Moon

Image Manager Manager Control: Absolutely no one

Artistic Arguer: Sunok Moon

Dishwasher: Matthew Hitch
(occasionally Sunok Moon)

Title: Captain Matt's Super Crazy Fun

Big Kid Phonics 5 Student Book

ISBN 979-11-93590-29-4

First published 2023

Published by Hitch Publishing

info@supercrazyfun.net



This textbook came about as the result of 20 years of trying to make kids enjoy learning English. It is designed around the use of the rhotic R and other characteristics of English pronunciation common in North America. We believe it can be used in other parts of the world as most phonics books can, and we are keen to hear feedback from anyone who tries this.

We want to make clear that the word "crazy" used in the title is in relation to any of the common definitions illustrated below, and does not refer in any way to the meaning "insane."

**strange/illogical**      **wild**      **unexpected**      **fun**      **unwise**

About the Authors:

Matthew Hitch has taught English in Korea for the better part of 20 years and holds a master's degree in applied linguistics. He clearly does not have a pig nose, and by most accounts is not at all malodorous. He also cuts a dashing figure according to his wife.

Sunok Moon prefers to go by the name Michelle, and is in fact quite scary as reported in the bio on the back of this book. She has a degree in English literature and has taught English in Korea for approximately 3 weeks longer than Matthew, who is writing this and finds it weird to refer to himself in the third person.

# Contents

# Welcome parents and teachers!

Thank you for considering our book. Phonics books are notoriously boring, so this is the last bastion of publishing where even the tiniest bit of creativity can raise the bar (sorry phonics book publishers, but it's true). With that said, we humbly offer you our content. We have also intentionally challenged convention in a few ways. Much of what we have to say may be used or discarded though, and these books can be used just like any other mainstream phonics book. We hope you will choose to use whatever you please and dispose of the rest.

Please allow us to explain just where our method of teaching phonics may diverge from mainstream approaches, and please do forgive us for sharing information from what is undeniably the most mind-numbingly boring and seemingly useless field of study, linguistics. Most phonics books are not written by scholars in the field of linguistics. They are mostly written by early childhood educators, so perhaps that's the first divergence. We'll start with how we sound out consonants. In linguistic studies it is not uncommon for consonants to be distinguished by using a vowel (usually "ah") on both sides. This means a "V" sounds like "ahvah" and an "F" sounds like "ahfah" and so on. Most phonics books distinguish consonant sounds without such preceding vowel, but they do follow with a vowel in the form of the schwa. This is fine for most consonants, but the ones that are able to be maintained until breath is exhausted can be confusing with a schwa where they end a word. It's mostly ESL students who feel this confusion, but we think it doesn't hurt to teach those consonants without a schwa to native speakers as well, so where "V" sounds like "və" in most phonics books, in our book it is presented as "vvvvvvv" with no schwa. We apply this to all long consonant sounds in our audio files (L,M,N&R are also presented as long with a tiny schwa sound at the end though). If you have read this far, we take our hats off to you. Most would be fast asleep by now.

The next divergence is our use of Magic E. We chose Magic E for the fun  potential. The Split Digraphs just can't seem to hold a crowd. Magic E is no longer used in most educational settings for many reasons, but mostly because as a rule it cannot be defined clearly. We do mention that split digraphs are better though, mainly to extend an olive branch to all the teachers we hope will buy our books.



And the final divergence we would like to mention is our choice of words. Our choice of words may seem a bit odd at times throughout the books, but we chose them for their potential for keeping kids engaged over their usefulness. We approach a phonics book as a tool to teach about sounds much more than vocabulary. Poop, vomit, spit, fart, snot, and burp are the most popular with our students. We tried to find a spot for booger, but alas...

Our word choice is also strange in that it includes words that have the long E vowel when teaching split digraphs. Most phonics books glance over the long E vowel. The argument we have heard for this is that it is difficult for the younger students, but we suspect that it's avoided more because it's difficult for authors to find suitable words. We decided to give it a try, and our experience is that the long E words we chose are not that difficult for our students to grasp. Given that English is their second language, we believe native English speaking kids will cope with them just fine. Also you may notice our sight words are not all actually sight words - oops! Anyway, we hope you enjoy our silly books.

# Welcome students!

Tracks 0-9

Now we will learn how to put letters together to make new vowel sounds. Sometimes we put vowel letters together, and sometimes vowel and consonant letters together. Making these new vowel sounds can be difficult.



We have to memorize lots of different sounds for many of the same pairs of letters. Sometimes it might feel impossible, but we can do it!

We have to memorize them because they don't make their usual sounds.
Sometimes it seems even THEY don't know what they're doing.

We can't control them. Our job is just to learn all the new sounds they make together.

Let's get started...

**Welcome Students!**    5

## Vowels

Let's practice them before we start.

Tracks 0-9

Track 5

| Name | short sound | |
|------|-------------|---|
| A | a | 😃 |
| E | e | 😃 |
| I | i | 😐 |
| O | o | 😕 |
| U | u | 😐 |

i and u can be VERY short!

Remember the consonant blends? Vowels also go together like that, but they don't blend quite as well as consonants. They usually make a whole new sound.

## Vowel Combinations

When vowels get together to make a new vowel sound they change and swap their sounds. It's very confusing. We have to use our memory a lot.

The funny thing about these new vowel sounds is that consonants can join in too! They all change their sounds like there are no rules, but there is one rule. Vowels are on the left and consonants are on the right!

Track
6

Tracks 0-9

Listen, point, and make the sound: 

Tracks 0-9

Words with ai, ay, ee, ea

Track 7

**1**  ai  ay

**2**  ea  ee

Listen, point, and say the word: 

Track 8

1  w + ait = wait  wait

2  tr + ee = tree  tree

3  d + ay = day  day

# Follow the rules   

## Write the words

1  **w** + **ait** = ________________ 

2  **tr** + **ee** = ________________ 

3  **d** + **ay** = ________________ 

4  **ea** + **t** = ________________ 

5  **s** + **ail** = ________________ 

6  **t** + **eeth** = ________________ 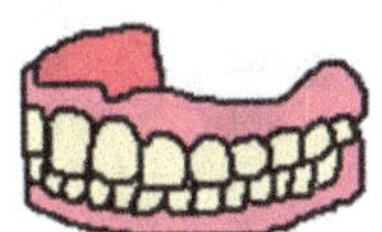

## Listen, point and repeat the new words

**ai**

sail     train     wait

**ay**

day     play     say

**ee**

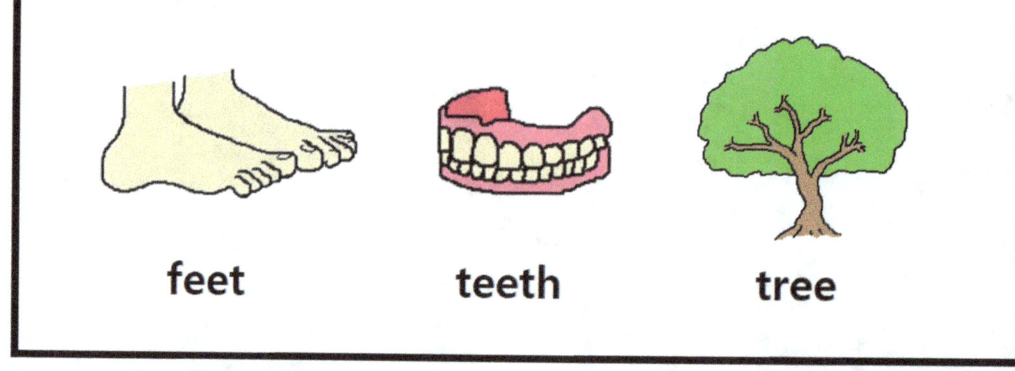

feet     teeth     tree

**ea**

eat     meat     teach

# Exercises

## Listen and write

Tracks 10-19

1 

2 

3 

4 

5 

6 

7 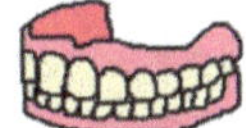

8 

9 

10 

11 

12 

## Listen and circle the right letters AND picture



1 ai ee ay ea 

2 ai ee ay ea 

3 ai ee ay ea 

4 ai ee ay ea 

5 ai ee ay ea 

6 ai ee ay ea 

**Unit 1    11**

# Exercises

## Circle the word you hear

Tracks 10-19

Track 12

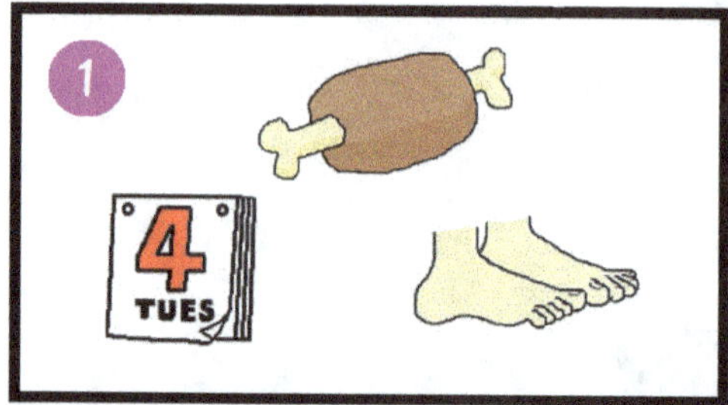  

## Circle the vowel sound you hear

Track 13

1. ai ee ay ea    2. ai ee ay ea

3. ai ee ay ea    4. ai ee ay ea

5. ai ee ay ea    6. ai ee ay ea

## Chant

Track 14

Sight words: way

I eat meat
With my feet
I do it every day
People say don't eat that way!
To eat that way is bad they say
But I eat meat
With my feet
I do it every day!

12    Unit 1

# Story

Track 15

Tracks 10-19

New words: mean slay sleep deep creep
near hear leap please how clean

# UNIT 2    Vowel Combinations

Listen, point, and make the sound:  Words with oa, ow, oi, oy

Tracks 10-19

Track 16

**1** oa ow

**2** oi oy

Listen, point, and say the word: Track 17

**1** b + oat = boat 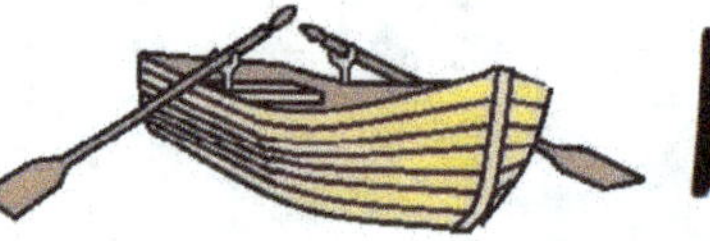 boat

**2** b + oil = boil  boil

**3** b + owl = bowl  bowl

# Follow the rules 

## Write the words

1  b + oat  = ___________ 

2  b + oil  = ___________ 

3  b + owl = ___________ 

4  b + oy  = ___________ 

5  c + oat = ___________ 

6  t + oilet = ___________ 

# New Words

Track 18

Tracks 10-19

## oa

| boat | coat | soap |

## ow

| bowl | slow | throw |

## oi

| boil | noise | toilet |

## oy

| boy | oyster | toy |

# Exercises

## Listen and write

Tracks 10-19

1 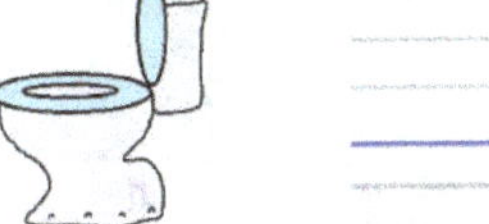 _______________    2 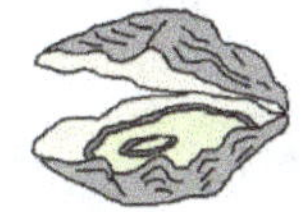 _______________

3  _______________    4  _______________

5  _______________    6  _______________

7  _______________    8  _______________

9  _______________    10  _______________

11  _______________    12  _______________

## Listen and circle the right letters AND picture



1 oa oi ow oy     2 oa oi ow oy 

3 oa oi ow oy     4 oa oi ow oy 

5 oa oi ow oy     6 oa oi ow oy 

# Exercises

## Circle the word you hear

## Circle the vowel sound you hear



1. oa  oi  ow  oy
2. oa  oi  ow  oy
3. oa  oi  ow  oy
4. oa  oi  ow  oy
5. oa  oi  ow  oy
6. oa  oi  ow  oy

## Chant



Boil oysters in a toilet
Boil oysters in a toilet
Boil oysters in a toilet
Put some soap in

Boil oysters in a toilet
Boil oysters in a toilet
Boil oysters in a toilet
Throw them in the bin

**18    Unit 2**

# Story

Track 24

Tracks 20-29

New words: mom  her  hair  took  gone  pass  annoy  sword

| | | |
|---|---|---|
| Deb Sailaway was very cute. | Deb's mom cut her hair with a bowl. | And Deb liked that. |

| | | |
|---|---|---|
| Deb also liked to sail toy boats. | She took her toy boat to the lake. | One boy was very mean. |

| | | |
|---|---|---|
| The boy's boat made a big noise. | And Deb's toy boat was gone. | 20 years passed. |

| | | |
|---|---|---|
| MOVE YOUR BOAT! | Ha ha! Your boat is too slow! | It was the same mean boy! Deb was really annoyed. |

| | | |
|---|---|---|
| She took the boy's sword. | And the boy's hat and coat. | And the boy's big boat, too! |

Listen, point, and make the sound:  Words with ou, ow, ar, or

Tracks 20-29

**Track 25**

1 **ou ow**

2 **ar**   3 **or**

Listen, point, and say the word: **Track 26**

1 h + **ou**se = h**ou**se  house

2 c + **ar** = c**ar**  car

3 h + **orn** = h**orn**  horn

# Follow the rules 

1  h + ouse =  _______________  

2  c + ar  =  _______________  

3  h + orn  =  _______________  

4  c + ow  =  _______________  

5  ou + t  =  _______________  

6  br + own =  _______________  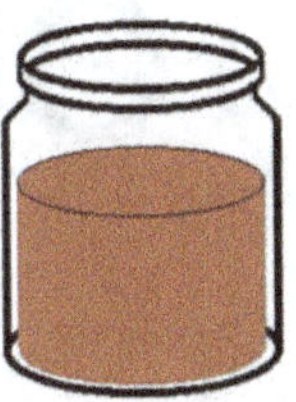

# New Words

## Listen, point and repeat the new words



## ou

| house | out | shout |

## ow

| brown | cow | owl |

## ar

| car | fart | shark |

## or

| corn | horn | short |

# Exercises

## Listen and write

1  _______________

2  _______________

3  _______________

4  _______________

5  _______________

6  _______________

7  _______________

8  _______________

9  _______________

10  _______________

11  _______________

12  _______________

## Listen and circle the right letters AND picture



1 ou ow ar or 

2 ou ow ar or 

3 ou ow ar or 

4 ou ow ar or 

5 ou ow ar or 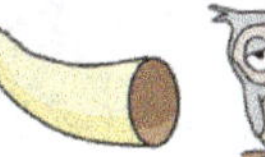

6 ou ow ar or 

# Exercises

## Circle the word you hear

Tracks 30-39

## Circle the vowel sound you hear

1  ou  ow  ar  or        2  ou  ow  ar  or

3  ou  ow  ar  or        4  ou  ow  ar  or

5  ou  ow  ar  or        6  ou  ow  ar  or

## Chant

Brown cows eating corn in a car
Did you fart?
Did you fart?
Get out of the car!



Brown cows eating corn in a house.
Did you fart?
Did you fart?
Get out of the house!

24    Unit 3

# Story

## Listen and read along

Tracks 30-39

New words: beach guard if every blow um

# Review

Listen and repeat all the words

Tracks 30-39

**1  ai / ay**

sail · train · wait

day · play · say

**2  ee / ea**

feet · teeth · tree

eat · meat · teach

**3  oa / ow**

boat · coat · soap

bowl · slow · throw

**4  oi / oy**

boil · noise · toilet

boy · oyster · toy

**5  ou / ow**

house · out · shout

brown · cow · owl

**6  ar / or**

car · fart · shark

corn · horn · short

# Review

Say the word and write it

1  ___________________

2  ___________________

3  ___________________

4  ___________________

5 ___________________

6 ___________________

7  ___________________

8  ___________________

9  ___________________

10  ___________________

11  ___________________

12  ___________________

Now put the numbers in the boxes according to sound

| ai/ay | oa/ow | ou/ow | oi/oy |
|---|---|---|---|
|  |  |  |  |

| ea/ee | ar | or | |
|---|---|---|---|
|  |  |  | When you finish the last one, make a fart noise and blame the teacher. **That was you!** |

## Long and Short Sounds

Tracks 30-39

When two vowels come together they might make a long vowel sound...

Track 35

...or they might make a SHORT one!

Track 36

Track 37

They are very unpredictable!

## Cool R

People say R is bossy, but we think maybe some vowels
feel it's so cool they just let it make all the noise.

Tracks 30-39

Track
38

## Oddball G

G is a funny one. It hangs around quietly in words and
does odd things to the the letters near it.

It likes to be with H. Sometimes when they're together it
makes the F sound, but not often.

Listen, point, and make the sound:  Words with oo, oo, ew, ue

1 **oo** SHORT

2 **oo ew ue**

Listen, point, and say the word: Track 40

1 c + ook = cook  cook

2 f + ood = food  food

3 ch + ew = chew  chew

# Follow the rules   

**Write the words**

1  c + ook = _______________ 

2  f + ood = _______________ 

3  ch + ew = _______________ 

4  bl + ue = _______________ 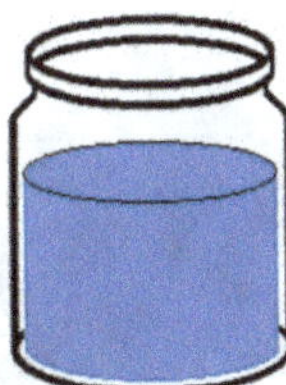

5  f + oot = _______________ 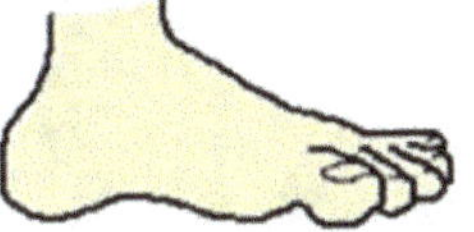

6  z + oo = _______________ 

# New Words

Tracks 40-49

Track 41

## oo (short)

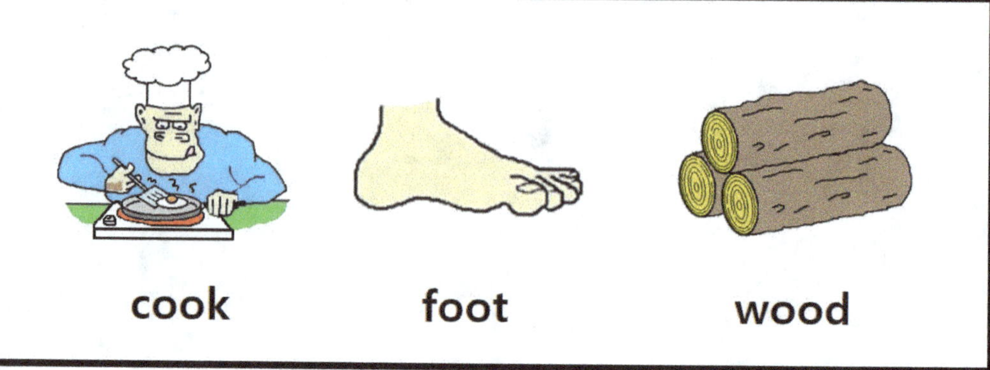

cook     foot     wood

## oo

food     pool     zoo

## ew

chew     new     stew

## ue

blue     clue     glue

# Exercises

## Listen and write

Tracks 40-49

1  _______________

2  _______________

3  _______________

4  _______________

5 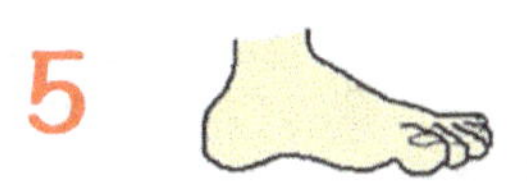 _______________

6  _______________

7  _______________

8 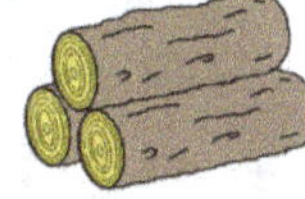 _______________

9  _______________

10  _______________

11  _______________

12  _______________

## Listen and circle the right letters AND picture



1 oo oo ew ue 
SHORT

2 oo oo ew ue 
SHORT

3 oo oo ew ue 
SHORT

4 oo oo ew ue 
SHORT

5 oo oo ew ue 
SHORT

6 oo oo ew ue 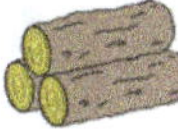
SHORT

**Unit 4**  33

# Exercises

## Circle the word you hear

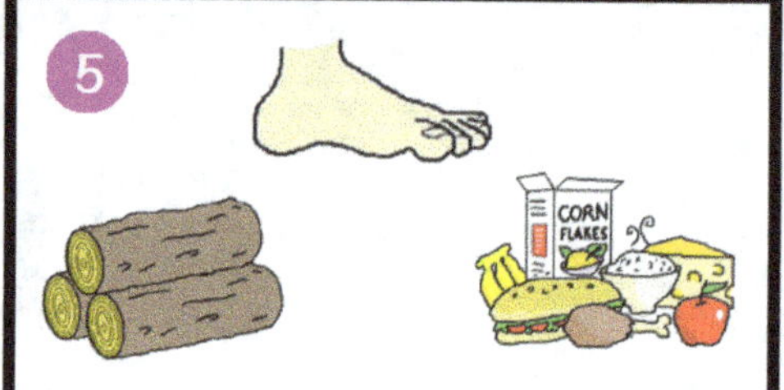
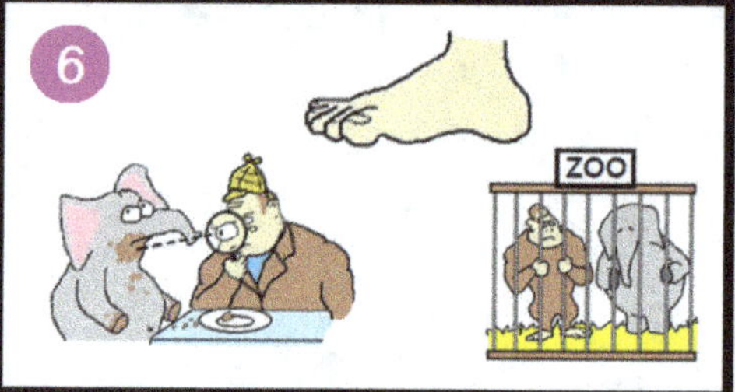

## Circle the vowel sound you hear



1. oo (SHORT)   oo   ew   ue
2. oo (SHORT)   oo   ew   ue
3. oo (SHORT)   oo   ew   ue
4. oo (SHORT)   oo   ew   ue
5. oo (SHORT)   oo   ew   ue
6. oo (SHORT)   oo   ew   ue

## Chant

Sight words: cannot



Don't put your foot in my food
Your foot I cannot chew

Don't put blue glue in my stew
I cannot chew blue glue

Foot in food, glue in stew
I cannot chew this food from you!

**34**    Unit 4

# Story

Track 47
Tracks 40-49

New words: cool who print live true know

Listen, point, and make the sound:  Words with er, ir, ur, or

**Tracks 40-49**

Track 48

1

er ir

or ur

Listen, point, and say the word:

Track 49

1 p + erm = perm  perm

2 g + irl = girl  girl

3 b + urp = burp  burp

# Follow the rules   

1  p + erm  = ___________  

2  g + irl  = ___________  

3  b + urp  = ___________  

4  w + ork  = ___________  

5  teach + er  = ___________  

6  doct + or  = ___________  

# New Words

## Listen, point and repeat the new words

**er**

germ | perm | teacher

**ir**

dirt | girl | stir

**or**

doctor | work | worm

**ur**

burp | fur | turn

# Exercises

## Listen and write



Tracks 50-59

1  ______________

2  ______________

3  ______________

4  ______________

5  ______________

6  ______________

7  ______________

8  ______________

9  ______________

10  ______________

11  ______________

12  ______________

## Listen and circle the right letters AND picture



1 er ir ur or 

2 er ir ur or 

3 er ir ur or 

4 er ir ur or 

5 er ir ur or 

6 er ir ur or 

# Exercises

## Circle the word you hear

Tracks 50-59

## Circle the vowel sound you hear



1. er  ir  ur  or          2. er  ir  ur  or

3. er  ir  ur  or          4. er  ir  ur  or

5. er  ir  ur  or          6. er  ir  ur  or

## Chant



Dirt and germs in my fur
My fur has dirt and germs
Dirt and worms in my perm
My perm has dirt and worms
Dirt and germs and fur and worms
Fur and worms and dirt and germs
Dirt and worms in my perm
My fur has dirt and germs

**40**   Unit 5

# Story

## Listen and read along

Extra words: would could head brew
surgery heed word proud about

**The Ship's Doctor**

Herbert Burger was a good doctor.

He lived and worked on a big boat.

Every day he would cure the sailors.

He could fix a bone.

Or fix a head.

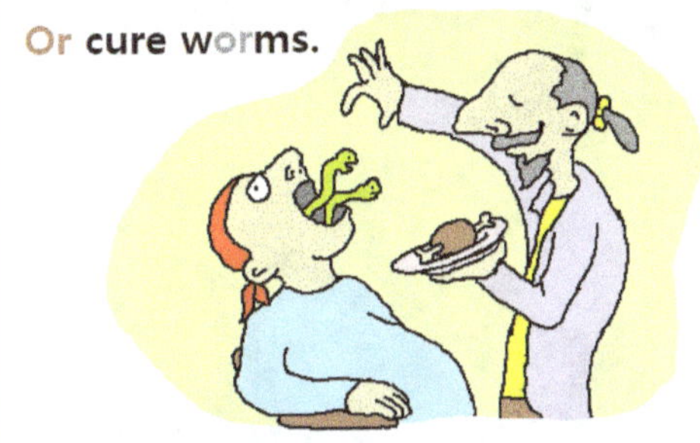
Or cure worms.

Or stir a brew to cure burps.

But his best work was surgery.

He would heed his teacher's words.

He was very proud of his surgery.

But he didn't know about germs.

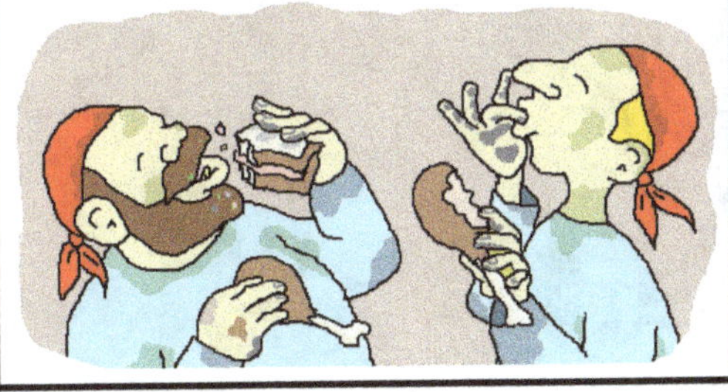
Everyone was very dirty.

Herbert was a happy doctor.

Then one day he turned his head
and saw a girl.

Listen, point, and make the sound:  Words with ou, ou, ie, igh

Tracks 50-59

Track 57

1 **ou**

2 **ou** SHORT

3 **ie**   **igh**

Listen, point, and say the word:

Track 58

1 y + ou = you  you

2 y + oung SHORT = young SHORT  young

3 l + ie = lie  lie

## Write the words

1  y + ou  = __________ 

2  y + oung = __________ 
SHORT

3  l + ie  = __________ 

4  s + oup = __________ 

5  t + ouch = __________ 
SHORT

6  f + ight = __________ 

# New Words

## Listen, point and repeat the new words

**ou**

group     soup     you

**ou** (short)

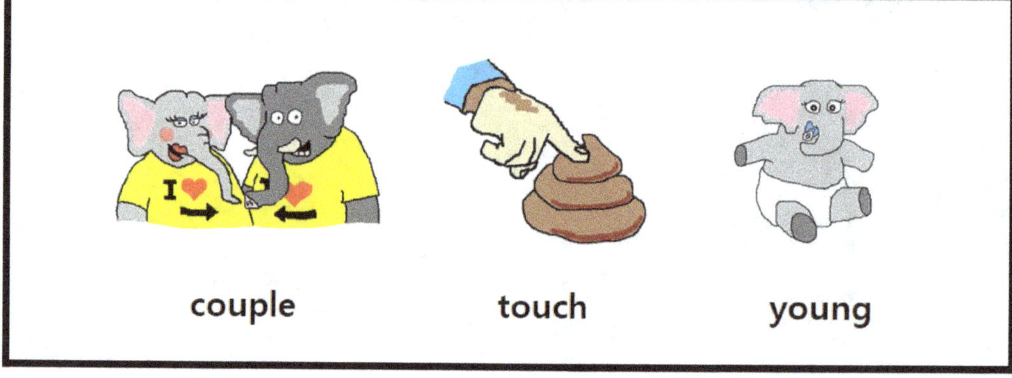

couple     touch     young

**ie**

lie     pie     tie

**igh**

fight     night     sigh

# Exercises

## Listen and write



1 

2 

3 

4 

5 

6 

7 

8 

9 

10 

11

12

## Listen and circle the right letters AND picture



1 ou ou ie igh  
SHORT

2 ou ou ie igh  
SHORT

3 ou ou ie igh  
SHORT

4 ou ou ie igh  
SHORT

5 ou ou ie igh  
SHORT

6 ou ou ie igh 
SHORT

Unit 6    45

## Circle the word you hear

## Circle the vowel sound you hear

1. ou   ou SHORT   ie   igh
2. ou   ou SHORT   ie   igh
3. ou   ou SHORT   ie   igh
4. ou   ou SHORT   ie   igh
5. ou   ou SHORT   ie   igh
6. ou   ou SHORT   ie   igh

## Chant

Sight words:  grab   join

Soup night, soup night
Group soup night
Grab some soup and join the group

Pie fight, pie fight
Group pie fight!
Grab a pie and join the fight

Pies and soup and fights at night
I like the group soup night pie fight!

# Story

## Listen and read along

# Review

Listen and repeat all the words

Tracks 60-69

**①  oo / oo**

| cook | foot | wood |
|------|------|------|
| food | pool | zoo |

**②  ew / ue**

| chew | new | stew |
|------|-----|------|
| blue | clue | glue |

**③  er / ir**

| germ | perm | teacher |
|------|------|---------|
| dirt | girl | stir |

**④  ur / or**

| burp | fur | turn |
|------|-----|------|
| doctor | work | worm |

**⑤  ou / ou**

| group | soup | you |
|-------|------|-----|
| couple | touch | young |

**⑥  ie / igh**

| lie | pie | tie |
|-----|-----|-----|
| fight | night | sigh |

# Review

Say the word and write it

1  _______________

2 _______________

3 _______________

4  _______________

5  _______________

6  _______________

7  _______________

8  _______________

9 _______________

10 _______________

11 _______________

12 _______________

Now put the numbers in the boxes according to sound

| ie igh | er ir | ew ue oo ou |
|---|---|---|

| oo | ou |
|---|---|

When you finish the last one, point to the teacher and shout:

**Wild gorilla! Call the zoo!**

Listen, point, and make the sound:  Words with ea, ea, ey, ey

Tracks 60-69

Track 67

1 **ea**　　**ey**

2 **ea**　3 **ey**

Listen, point, and say the word:

Track 68

1 st + **ea**k = st**ea**k  steak

2 br + **ea**d = br**ea**d   bread

3 k + **ey** = k**ey**  key

## Write the words

1  st + **eak** = __________  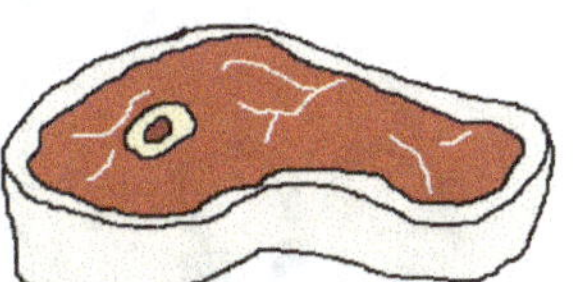

2  br + **ead** = __________  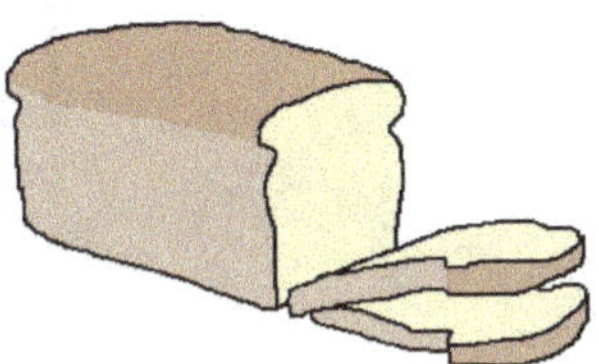

3  k + **ey** = __________  

4  gr + **eat** = __________  

5  sw + **eat** = __________  

6  h + **ey** = __________  

# New Words

## Listen, point and repeat the new words

**ea** (short)

bread    health    sweat

**ea**

break    great    steak



**ey**

hey    obey    prey

**ey**

honey    key    money

## Listen and write

Tracks 70-79

1 

2    

3  

4  

5  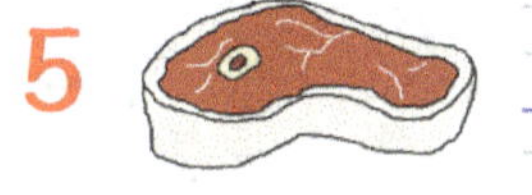

6 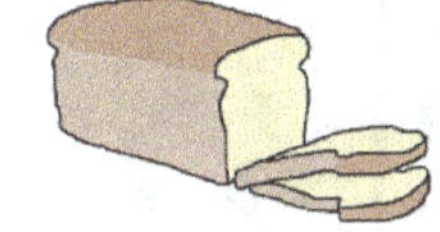

7 

8 

9 

10 

11 

12 

## Listen and circle the right letters AND picture



1 ea  ea SHORT  ey   

2 ea  ea SHORT  ey  

3 ea  ea SHORT  ey  

4 ea  ea SHORT  ey   

5 ea  ea SHORT  ey   

6 ea  ea SHORT  ey  

**Unit 7**   53

# Exercises

## Circle the word you hear

Tracks 70-79

## Circle the vowel sound you hear



1  ea   ea SHORT   ey          2  ea   ea SHORT   ey

3  ea   ea SHORT   ey          4  ea   ea SHORT   ey

5  ea   ea SHORT   ey          6  ea   ea SHORT   ey

## Chant



Extra words: slice

Hey! Hey! You must obey!
Don't break the bread that way.

Silce it nicely, that's the key!
Don't just break it,
Can't you see?

Hey! Hey! You must obey!
Don't break the bread that way.

## Listen and read along

**Extra words:** job  lot  pay  beast  weapon  deadly  bear  valley

| | | |
|---|---|---|
| Get ready for a great new job! | Have the key to the health club. | You need to be healthy and strong. |
| You must eat a lot of steak... | ...and sweat a lot every day. | But I will pay you a lot of money! |
| This time you will hunt a wild beast! | Your prey is the great scary... | ...wild, mean, huge, angry... |
| ...honey-bee! | You will need big weapons. | Hey! This is no joke! It is deadly! |
| The Great Honey-Bee has a huge head! | It is like a bear! | Later, in a deep valley... |

Listen, point, and make the sound: | Track 76 |   Words with *ie, ei, oe, ui*

**Tracks 70-79**

1  ie  ei

2  oe   3  ui

Listen, point, and say the word: | Track 77 |

1  th + ief = thief   thief

2  t + oe = toe   toe

3  j + uice = juice 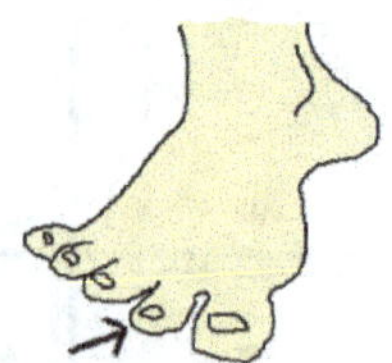  juice

## Write the words

1  th + ief  =  ___________ 

2  t + oe  =  ___________ 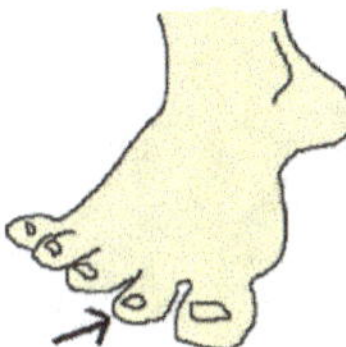

3  j + uice  =  ___________ 

4  fr + uit  =  ___________ 

5  al + oe  =  ___________ 

6  wei + rd  =  ___________ 

# New Words

Listen, point and repeat the new words

Track 78

**ui**

fruit     juice     suit

**oe**

aloe     oboe     toe

**ie**

genie     movie     thief

**ei**

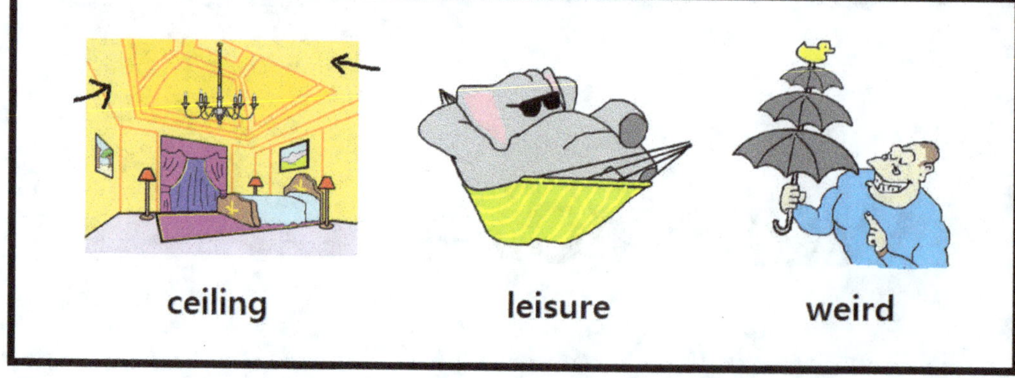

ceiling     leisure     weird

# Exercises

## Listen and write

1     _______________________

2     _______________________

3     _______________________

4     _______________________

5     _______________________

6     _______________________

7     _______________________

8     _______________________

9     _______________________

10     _______________________

11     _______________________

12     _______________________

## Listen and circle the right letters AND picture



1   ui   oe   ie   ei  

2   ui   oe   ie   ei  

3   ui   oe   ie   ei

4   ui   oe   ie   ei  

5   ui   oe   ie   ei

6   ui   oe   ie   ei  

# Exercises

## Circle the word you hear

Tracks 80-89

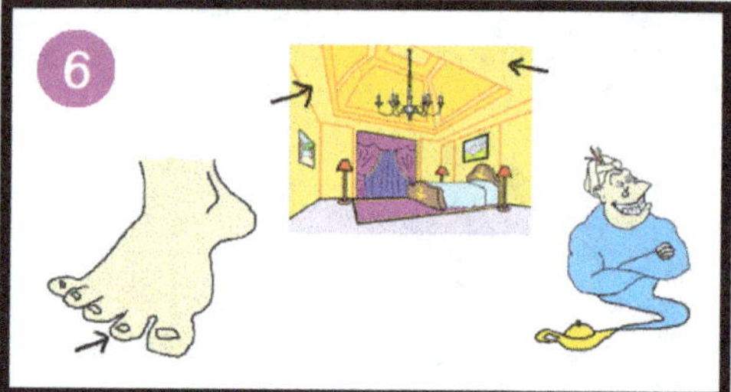

## Circle the vowel sound you hear

1. ui   oe   ie   ei        2. ui   oe   ie   ei

3. ui   oe   ie   ei        4. ui   oe   ie   ei

5. ui   oe   ie   ei        6. ui   oe   ie   ei

## Chant

Sight words: why

Weird genie in a suit,
Plays the oboe.
Weird genie eating fruit,
Plays the oboe.
Why does he wear a suit?
Why is he eating fruit?
Why is he in a lute?
I don't know-boe!

## Listen and read along

dear  help  whack  receive
gum  tight  watch

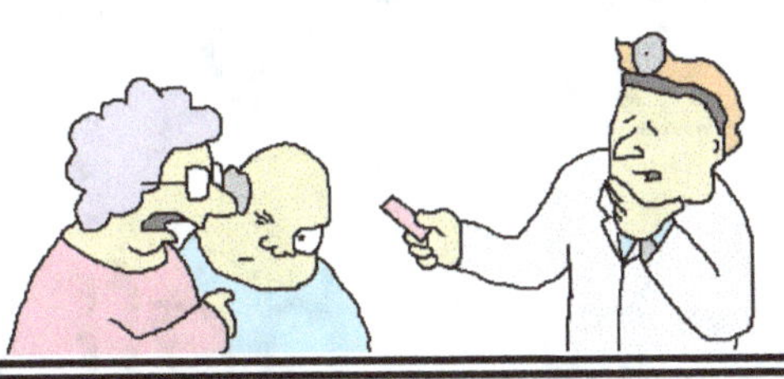

Listen, point, and make the sound:  Words with *ei, a, au, aw*

Tracks 80-89

Track 85

1 **ei**

2 **al au aw**

Listen, point, and say the word: Track 86

1 **ei** + **ght** = **ei**ght  eight

2 b + **all** = b**all**  ball

3 s + **aw** = s**aw**  saw

# Follow the rules   

**Write the words**

1   ei + ght  = _______________   8

2   b + all  = _______________   

3   s + aw  = _______________   

4   v + eil  = _______________   

5   t + alk  = _______________   

6   h + aunt  = _______________   

# New Words

## Listen, point and repeat the new words

Track 87

**ei**

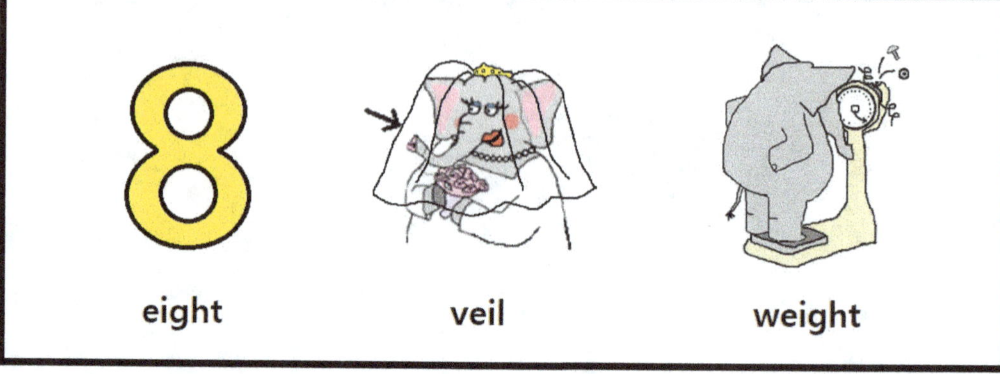

eight     veil     weight

**al**

ball     talk     tall

**au**

August     haunt     sauce

**aw**

crawl     saw     yawn

# Exercises

## Listen and write





1 __________

2 __________

3 __________

4 __________

5 __________

6 __________

7 __________

8 __________

9 __________

10 __________

11 __________

12 __________

## Listen and circle the right letters AND picture



1 ei al au aw 

2 ei al au aw 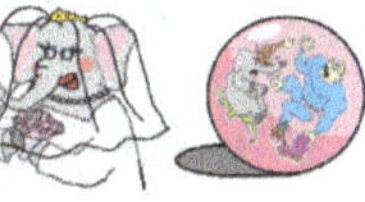

3 ei al au aw 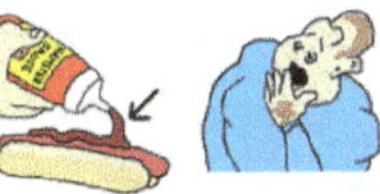

4 ei al au aw 

5 ei al au aw 

6 ei al au aw  

# Exercises

## Circle the word you hear

Tracks 90-99

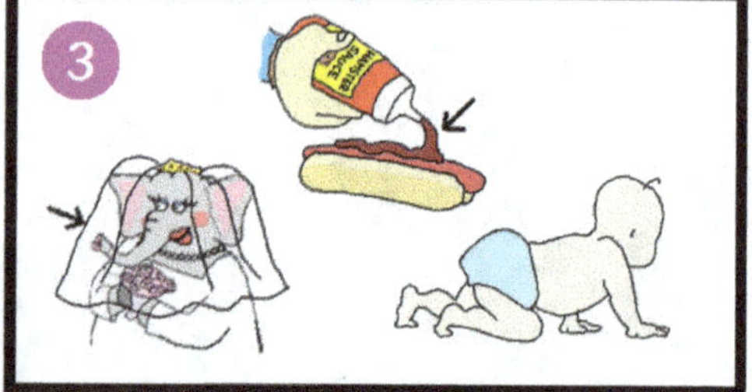

## Circle the vowel sound you hear

1   ei al au aw    2   ei al au aw

3   ei al au aw    4   ei al au aw

5   ei al au aw    6   ei al au aw

## Chant



I saw you talk and talk and talk,
For eight days in August.
You saw me yawn and yawn and yawn,
For eight days in August.
I saw you talk, you saw me yawn,
Talk talk talk and yawn yawn yawn,
I saw you talk and talk and talk,
For eight days in August.

# Story

Track
93

Tracks 90-99

lord  awful  fault  taught  where  until  dawn
were  buy  floor  draw  chalk  haul  ladder

# Review

Listen and repeat all the words

Track
94

Tracks 90-99

**1  ea/ea**

bread   health   sweat

break   great   steak

**2  ey/ey**

hey   obey   prey

honey   key   money

**3  ui/oe**

fruit   juice   suit

aloe   oboe   toe

**4  ie/ei**

genie   movie   thief

ceiling   leisure   weird

**5  ei/al**

eight   veil   weight

ball   talk   tall

**6  au/aw**

August   haunt   sauce

crawl   saw   yawn

# Review

Say the word and write it

1
2
3
4
5
6
7
8
9
10
11
12

Now put the numbers in the boxes according to sound

## Finished

Well, you have rounded up
and memorized all the new
vowel sounds this book has.

**Good job!**

**Now what will you do with them?**

## English is Bizzare

We haven't learnt everything though. Words can be very strange indeed.  Some words don't seem to make sense! We just have to memorize those ones.

Vowel combinations can change their sound on a whim, it seems. And so many letters are silent!

It really seems daunting, but now you know enough to see you through!

# Review

Circle the right sound

Tracks 90-99

1  ie er

2  oo oa

3 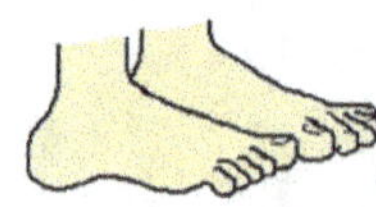 ou ee

4  al er

5  ey ar

6  ea ey

7  or ai

8 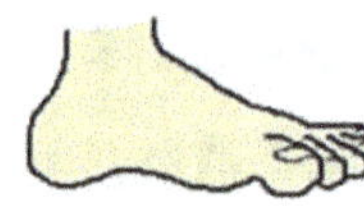 oo igh

9  ou ea

10  ee ai

11  oo ou

12  igh oy

13  oy ea

14  oi ou

15  ou ea

16  ou igh

17  ie or

18  ai ar

# Review

## Say the word and write it

1  _______________

2  _______________

3  _______________

4  _______________

5 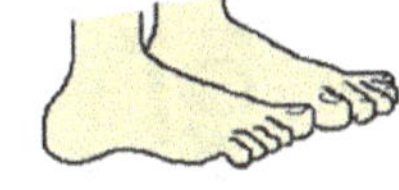 _______________

6  _______________

7  _______________

8  _______________

9  _______________

10  _______________

11  _______________

12  _______________

13  _______________

14  _______________

15  _______________

16  _______________

17 _______________

18  _______________

# Review

Say the words, and then write them in the right boxes below

you ng
h ou se
s ou p

br ea k
t ea ch
h ea lth

b ow l
br ow n

h or n
w or k

h ey
k ey

p ie
th ie f

w ei rd
v ei l

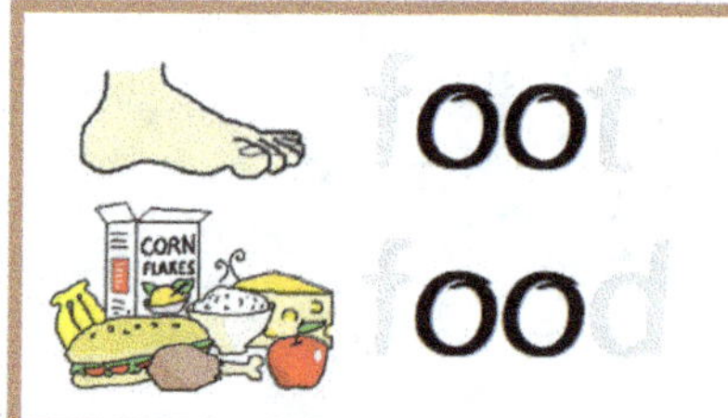

f oo t
f oo d

| ea ie ei ey | ou ow | ow | oo ou | oo |
| --- | --- | --- | --- | --- |

| | ie | ea ei ey | or | ea |
| --- | --- | --- | --- | --- |

| | or | | | ou |
| --- | --- | --- | --- | --- |

# Review

Track 98

Tracks 90-99

**1**
1 sail 2 train 3 wait 4 day 5 play 6 say
7 feet 8 teeth 9 tree 10 eat 11 meat 12 teach

**2**
1 boat 2 coat 3 soap 4 bowl 5 slow 6 throw
7 boil 8 noise 9 toilet 10 boy 11 oyster 12 toy

**3**
1 house 2 out 3 shout 4 brown 5 cow 6 owl
7 car 8 fart 9 shark 10 corn 11 horn 12 short

**4**
1 cook 2 foot 3 wood 4 food 5 pool 6 zoo
7 chew 8 new 9 stew 10 blue 11 clue 12 glue

**5**
1 germ 2 perm 3 teacher 4 dirt 5 girl 6 stir
7 doctor 8 work 9 worm 10 burp 11 fur 12 turn

**6**
1 group 2 soup 3 you 4 couple 5 touch 6 young
7 lie 8 pie 9 tie 10 fight 11 night 12 sigh

**7**
1 bread 2 health 3 sweat 4 break 5 great 6 steak
7 hey 8 obey 9 prey 10 honey 11 key 12 money

**8**
1 fruit 2 juice 3 suit 4 aloe 5 oboe 6 toe
7 genie 8 movie 9 thief 10 ceiling 11 leisure 12 weird

**9**
1 eight 2 veil 3 weight 4 ball 5 talk 6 tall
7 August 8 haunt 9 sauce 10 crawl 11 saw 12 yawn

# Test

## Listen and circle the word you hear  a  b  c 

**1**     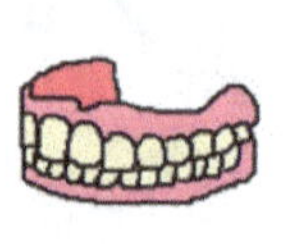  

**2**    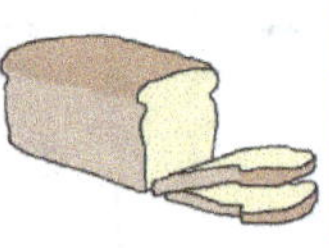   

**3**      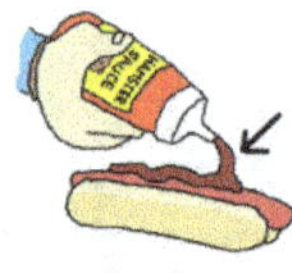 

**4**       

**5**      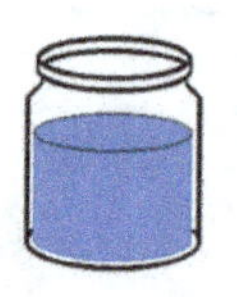 

**6**   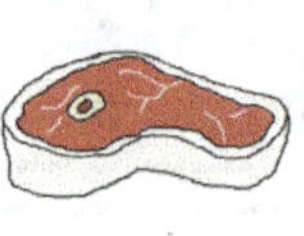   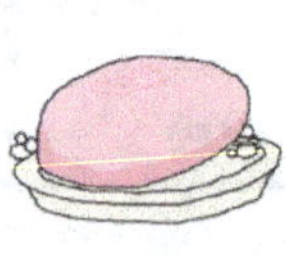 

**7**   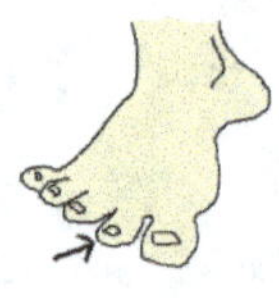    

# Test

Listen and write ANY digraph that matches  a  b  c 

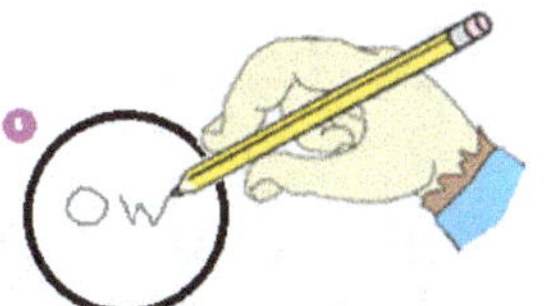

Tracks 100-110

1 ◯  2 ◯  3 ◯  4 ◯

5 ◯  6 ◯  7 ◯  8 ◯

9 ◯  10 ◯  11 ◯  12 ◯

13 ◯  14 ◯  15 ◯  16 ◯

# Test

Listen and circle the right combination a [Track 105] b [Track 106] c [Track 107]

Tracks 100-101

1  ou ee ai igh oe

2  ew ow oa al ui

3  oy ie ay aw or

4  er ei ey oo ar

5  ee au or oi oo

6  ur ea ou ue ey

# Test

## Circle the right sound

1  **ai oy**

2  **ou ea**

3  **oo oa**

4  **oy ea**

5  **ey ow**

6  **ey ar**

7  **or ai**

8  **oo igh**

9  **ou ue**

10  **ee ir**

11  **oo ou**

12  **oo igh**

13  **oi ea**

14  **aw ou**

15  **ey ar**

16  **ui igh**

17 **ie or**

18 **ea ey**

# This is the end of the series!

Miller Gorilla

Eloise Elephant

Isard Lizard

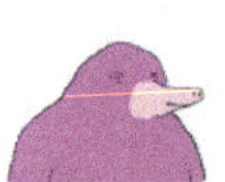

Noel Mole

Ludvig Pig

Sylvester fly

Debora Zebra

Reinhold Rhino

Eva Retriever

Peter Anteater

Steven Beaver

Luca Beluga

Matthew Hitch

Sunok Moon

# Word List

## Unit 1

sail

train

wait

day

play

say

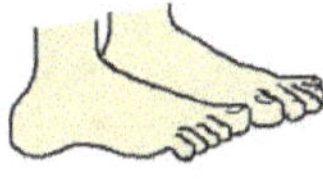
feet

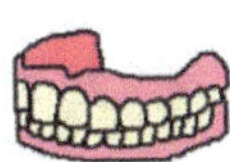
teeth

tree

eat

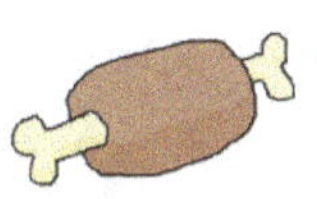
meat

teach

## Unit 2

boat

coat

soap

bowl

slow

throw

boil

noise

toilet

boy

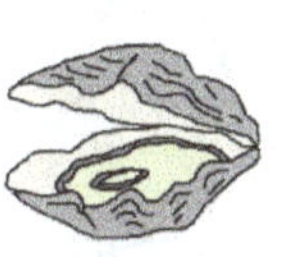
oyster

toy

## Unit 3

house

out

shout

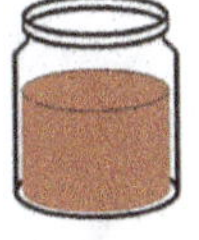
brown

cow

owl

car

fart

shark

corn

horn

short

# Word List

**Unit 4**

cook

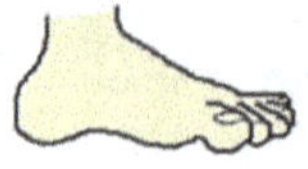
foot

wood

food

pool

zoo

chew

new

stew

blue

clue

glue

**Unit 5**

germ

perm

teacher

dirt

girl

stir

doctor

work

worm

burp

fur

turn

**Unit 6**

group

soup

you

couple

touch

young

lie

pie

tie

fight

night

sigh

# Word List

## Unit 7

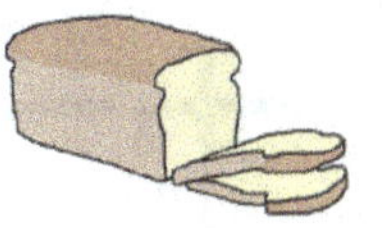
bread

health

sweat

break

great

steak

hey

obey

prey

honey

key

money

## Unit 8

fruit

juice

suit

aloe

oboe

toe

genie

movie

thief

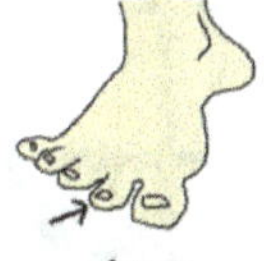
ceiling

leisure

weird

## Unit 9

eight

veil

weight

ball

talk

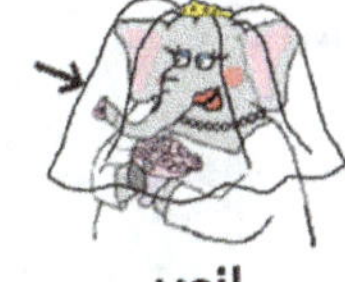
tall

August

haunt

sauce

crawl

saw

yawn

# Our Sight Words

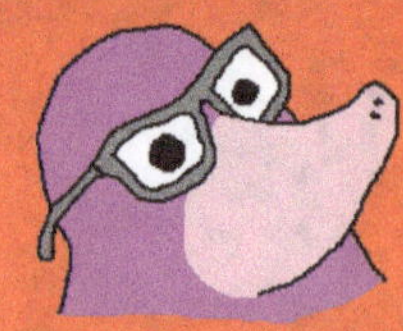

| Word | Note (ESL) | Word | Note (ESL) |
| --- | --- | --- | --- |
| a/an | | by | |
| and | | fellow | |
| all | | say | |
| on | | go | |
| in | | to | |
| the | | win | |
| no | | I | |
| lift | | had | |
| like | | it | |
| get | | wait | |
| oh | | have | |
| not | | that | |
| did | | yummy | |
| you | | what | |
| your | | she | |
| yes | | wear | |
| my | | so | |
| has | | scary | |
| put | | will | |
| one | | fell | |

# Our Sight Words

| Word | Note (ESL) | Word | Note (ESL) |
| --- | --- | --- | --- |
| down | | many | |
| am/are | | with | |
| want | | call | |
| give | | must | |
| me | | now | |
| him | | need | |
| shut | | maybe | |
| he | | don't | |
| handsome | | play | |
| pretty | | take | |
| let's | | us | |
| okay | | first | |
| talk | | brush | |
| do | | bake | |
| or | | with | |
| cent | | this | |
| stop | | we | |
| see | | whose | |
| too | | make | |
| them | | new | |

# Our Sight Words

| Word | Note (ESL) | Word | Note (ESL) |
|---|---|---|---|
| be | | lit | |
| best | | people | |
| can | | yell | |
| leave | | his | |
| at | | poem | |
| but | | into | |
| after | | birthday | |
| even | | walk | |
| next | | maid | |
| hello | | never | |
| for | | look | |
| home | | T-Rex | |
| room | | everyone | |
| only | | come | |
| also | | from | |
| can't | | onto | |
| is | | sir | |
| ate | | move | |
| still | | make | |
| soup | | some | |

# Our Sight Words

| Word | Note (ESL) | Word | Note (ESL) |
| --- | --- | --- | --- |
| slime | | really | |
| slide | | bring | |
| later | | welcome | |
| ready | | sorrry | |
| glue | | sneeze | |
| thing | | P12 way | |
| again | | mean | |
| check | | slay | |
| very | | sleep | |
| just | | deep | |
| should | | creep | |
| whole | | near | |
| wow | | hear | |
| choke | | leap | |
| aim | | please | |
| suit | | how | |
| smash | | clean | |
| as | | P19 mom | |
| our | | her | |
| guest | | hair | |

# Our Sight Words

| Word | Note (ESL) | Word | Note (ESL) |
|---|---|---|---|
| took | | head | |
| gone | | brew | |
| pass | | surgery | |
| annoy | | heed | |
| sword | | word | |
| P25 beach | | proud | |
| guard | | about | |
| if | | P46 grab | |
| every | | join | |
| blow | | beautiful | |
| um | | heart | |
| P34 cannot | | just | |
| cool | | last | |
| who | | right | |
| print | | marry | |
| live | | P54 slice | |
| true | | job | |
| know | | lot | |
| P41 would | | pay | |
| could | | beast | |

# Our Sight Words

| Word | Note (ESL) | Word | Note (ESL) |
|---|---|---|---|
| weapon | | draw | |
| deadly | | chalk | |
| bear | | haul | |
| valley | | ladder | |
| P60 why | | | |
| dear | | | |
| help | | | |
| whack | | | |
| gum | | | |
| tight | | | |
| watch | | | |
| P66 lord | | | |
| awful | | | |
| taught | | | |
| where | | | |
| until | | | |
| dawn | | | |
| were | | | |
| buy | | | |
| floor | | | |

# Phonics Series

## Preschool:

 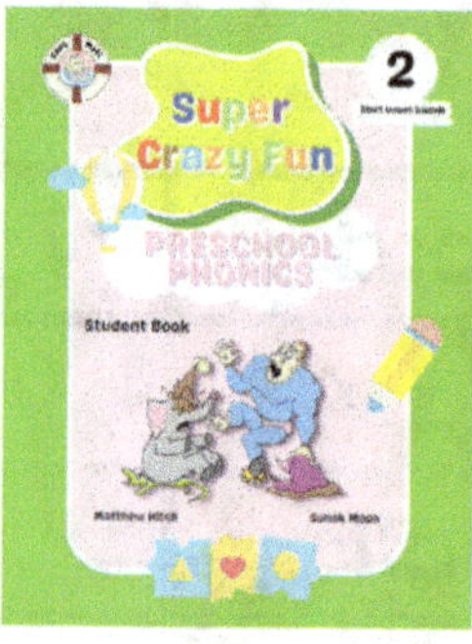   

## Kindergarten:

## Elementary School Junior:

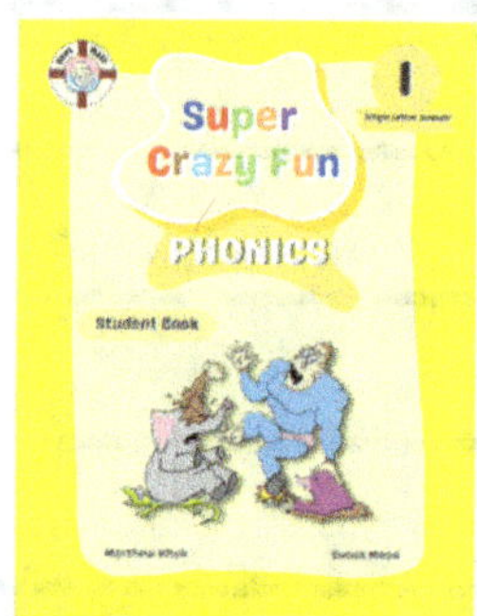    

## Elementary School Senior/Remedial:

Incidentally, the contents of all these phonics books are available in one big silly book, too:

Have a look in Amazon or check our website: www.supercrazyfun.net (or just search online in case our publishing options have increased since this was printed.)

# To parents and teachers:

This is one of 2 pages needed to fill up space due to uneven page numbers and printing requirements. If I didn't want to shamelessly tout our books on the previous two pages it wouldn't be an issue, but here we are. The co-author, who is also my dear wife, tollerantly rolls her eyes at my inclusion of silly things like this to fill space, so these ramblings are mine alone.

I'll use the space to connect with our other audience, you fine people We have been teaching using these books in our little English school in South Korea for a few years at the time of publishing this edition, and I'm not shy in saying I've not had children respond to phonics books before in the way they have responded to these books. I have never seen kids enthusiastically looking ahead in a phonics book to see what will happen next, and that has been the response. This inspired me to get these out of our little school and into your hands.

I sincerely thank you for trying them with so many already well-established phonics books currently available.

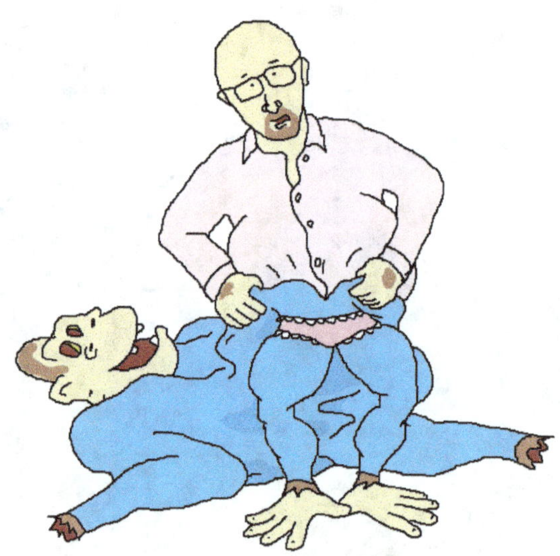

Matthew Hitch

(P.S. As you might have guessed, I identify with the gorilla in these books, and although my wife provided the voice for the elephant in all the audio files, I feel pressed to mention she definitely does not identify there at all, and that the pink frilly panties are a reference to the general Korean amusement at superheroes inexplicably wearing underpants outside their clothes; I do not do this.)

There's nothing on this page...


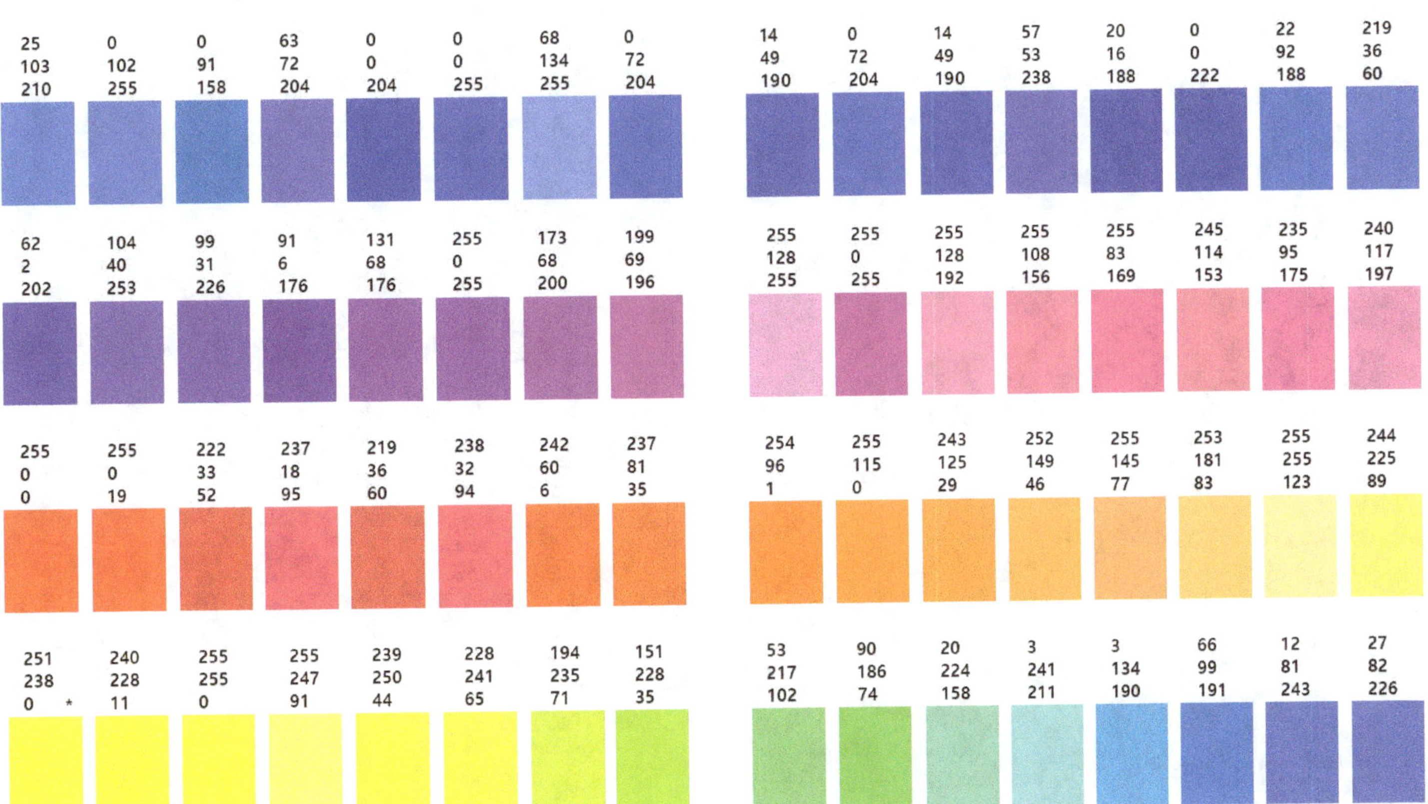

25 103 210
0 102 255
0 91 158
63 72 204
0 0 204
0 0 255
68 134 255
0 72 204
14 49 190
0 72 204
14 49 190
57 53 238
20 16 188
0 0 222
22 92 188
219 36 60
62 2 202
104 40 253
99 31 226
91 6 176
131 68 176
255 0 255
173 68 200
199 69 196
255 128 255
255 0 255
255 128 192
255 108 156
255 83 169
245 114 153
235 95 175
240 117 197
255 0 0
255 0 19
222 33 52
237 18 95
219 36 60
238 32 94
242 60 6
237 81 35
254 96 1
255 115 0
243 125 29
252 149 46
255 145 77
253 181 83
255 255 123
244 225 89
251 238 0 *
240 228 11
255 255 0
255 247 91
239 250 44
228 241 65
194 235 71
151 228 35
53 217 102
90 186 74
20 224 158
3 241 211
3 134 190
66 99 191
12 81 243
27 82 226